SIMPLY *SWEDISH*

SIMPLY
SWEDISH

STADT HAMBURGSGATAN 9B
211 38 MALMÖ, SWEDEN

IDEA & RECIPES: Margareta Schildt-Landgren
PHOTOGRAPHY: Tine Guth-Linse
PROSE POEMS: Carin Stentorp
IDEA & DESIGN: Helena Åkesson-Liedberg
PRINTED BY: Göteborgstryckeriet, 2009

ISBN 978-91-976190-5-9

Meatballs, cream buns, fresh berries, but also pike and chutney.

My aim has been to write an innovative cookery book with our fantastic Swedish produce as the main ingredients.

At times the food memories of my childhood have made themselves felt, but my life with food has absorbed influences from many quarters. The result is a mixture of traditional Swedish food and recipes with ingredients that have only recently been available in Sweden.

It is important for me to convey simplicity. My recipes are therefore easy to follow, and the ingredients can be found in most shops, sometimes depending on the season.

One thing at least is certain: it's fun to work with choice ingredients.

Margareta Schildt–Landgren

CONTENTS

the open landscape

A wind towards evening eases the heat over the fields.
The cool breeze carries the sound of iron bells,
calling us to rest for the coming Sunday.

VEAL IN DILL

This is a classical and very tasty Sunday dinner. Let the veal boil during the day, giving you time to do other things. That makes this meal really easy to prepare.

SERVES 4

1.2 kg VEAL WITH BONE
1 ONION
1+3 CARROTS
2 BAY LEAVES
1 teaspoon SALT
approx. 20 WHITE PEPPER CORNS
1 BUNCH OF DILL SPRIGS
approx. 12 POTATOES
3 tablespoons CORNFLOUR
2 tablespoons VEAL FOND
1 tablespoon LEMONJUICE
1 tablespoon RAPE-SEED OIL

Put the meat in a saucepan and pour on cold water so that it just covers the meat. Peel and halve the onion, and peel and divide a carrot. Put both onion and carrot in the pan together with bay leaves, salt and pepper corns. Add dill sprigs. Chop and save the actual dill crowns. Cover and boil over a low heat for approx. 1 hour until the meat comes free from the bone.

Take out the meat and let it cool slightly before cutting it into pieces.

Peel and boil the potatoes and carrots in lightly salted water.

Strain the stock from the meat and pour into another saucepan. Stir in the flour and let the sauce come to the boil. Stir in fond and lemon-juice to taste. Use a mixer to combine the dill crowns with a little oil. Stir them into the sauce. Put the meat in the sauce to heat it and then serve with boiled potatoes and carrots.

MEADOW FOOD

A wonderful name for a wonderful soup, made from the very first spring vegetables. You can also use other early vegetables, depending on availability and preferences.

SERVES 4

8 YOUNG CARROTS

8 SMALL FRESH POTATOES

1 SMALL HEAD OF CAULIFLOWER

100 g FRESH SPINACH

100 g SUGAR PEAS

4 SPRING ONIONS (SALAD ONIONS)

600 ml WATER

3 tablespoons VEGETABLE FOND

400 ml MILK

SALT AND PEPPER

100 ml COOKING CREAM

1 EGG YOLK

50 ml CHOPPED PARSLEY

Clean and brush the carrots and the potatoes. Cut the cauliflower into florets. Clean the spinach, the sugar peas and the spring onions, which may be cut into smaller pieces.

Boil water, fond and milk and gradually put in all the vegetables except the spinach, depending on how long they need to cook. Season and finally add the spinach. Mix the cream and yolk and pour gently into the soup, which should not be boiling or the cream will curdle. Sprinkle with chopped parsley.

GHERKINS IN NUTMEG AND HORSERADISH

In late summer you can buy small green gherkins at the market. When pickled with nutmeg flower and horseradish they are tasty with any dish that normally includes pickled gherkins, such as roasts.

Pour water in a bucket and add so much salt that a whole raw egg floats when you put it in.

Wash the gherkins and put them in the brine for 24 hours.

Pour sugar, 1 l water and acetic acid in a saucepan and bring to the boil. Let it cool completely.

Take the gherkins out of the brine and put them in large jars in layers alternating with mustard seeds, white pepper corns, nutmeg flowers, heads of dill and a little horseradish. If the horseradish is very pungent, use a smaller quantity. If the gherkins are big, prick them with a needle or else they will become slightly hollow.

Seal the lids and store for about 14 days before they are ready to eat.

APPROX. 3 KG

SALT FOR THE BRINE

3 kg SMALL, GREEN GHERKINS

750 g SUGAR

1 litre WATER

36 cl ACETIC ACID, 24%

50 g WHOLE YELLOW MUSTARD SEEDS

1/2 teaspoon WHOLE WHITE PEPPER CORNS

1/2 teaspoon NUTMEG FLOWER

7 HEADS OF DILL

2 cm PEELED FRESH HORSERADISH

SYRUP LOAF

We Swedes are rather unique in baking bread with syrup. This syrup loaf is the kind of bread that is most frequently found on the Swedish breakfast table.

Crumble the yeast in a bowl.

Add the margarine, the water, vinegar essence, salt, syrup and spices. Mix everything together well. Work in the rye flour so that the dough cleans the bowl. Allow to rise under cover in a draught-free place at room temperature for approx. 1 hour.

Place the dough on the table and knead it until it is smooth and elastic. Cut the dough into 2 equal-sized bits and shape into loaves. Put the loaves on oven paper and allow to rise for a further 45 minutes or so. Preheat the oven to 175 degrees. Bake in the lower half of the oven for approx. 40 minutes until the loaves sound hollow when you tap them on the bottom.

Brush the finished loaves with water. Allow to cool on a rack.

2 LOAVES

50 g SWEET DOUGH YEAST
50 ml LIQUID MARGARINE
500 ml LUKEWARM WATER
1/2 tablespoon VINEGAR ESSENCE
1 teaspoon SALT
100 ml LIGHT BREAD SYRUP
1 tablespoon SPICE MIX FOR BREAD
approx. 1500 ml SIFTED RYE FLOUR

At harvest time the kitchen is filled with the earthy steam coming from root vegetables.

We have time for a cup of coffee while the vinegar is boiling.

REINDEER STEW WITH ALMOND POTATO PURÉE AND CLOUDBERRY

Thinly sliced reindeer meat is bought frozen and the meat can be cooked at once, without being thawed. Together with the chanterelles, this is a rich stew that goes well with the mild taste of the potato purée, made from the small almond-shaped potatoes of northern Sweden.

Peel and chop the onion. Fry it in butter over a low heat until it is transparent.

Take out the onion and fry the chanterelles and sliced reindeer over a higher heat. Crush and add the juniper berries and blend in gin, crème fraîche and the fried onion. Season.

Peel the potatoes and boil until they disintegrate in lightly salted water. Pour off the water and mash. Add the cream and blend in the parsley.

Add salt and pepper to taste.

Serve with a dollop of cloudberry jam.

SERVES 4

1 ONION
1 tablespoon BUTTER
200 ml CHANTERELLES
300 g THINLY SLICED REINDEER MEAT
5 JUNIPER BERRIES
2 tablespoons GIN
200 ml CRÈME FRAÎCHE
SALT AND PEPPER
approx. 15 ALMOND POTATOES
100 ml MEDIUM-FAT CREAM
100 ml CHOPPED PARSLEY
4 tablespoons CLOUDBERRY JAM

LAMB-STUFFED CABBAGE LEAVES

This is a new way to stuff cabbage leaves. The use of savoy cabbage and minced lamb turns this everyday Swedish dish into a feast.

SERVES 4

100 ml JASMINE RICE

2 1/2 teaspoons SALT

1 HEAD OF SAVOY CABBAGE

3 SHALLOTS

500 g MINCED LAMB

1 CLOVE OF GARLIC

50 g GOAT'S MILK CHEESE

3 measuring spoons FRESHLY GROUND BLACK PEPPER

2 tablespoons RAPE-SEED OIL TO BRUSH WITH

1 tin WHOLE TOMATOES

10 ALMOND POTATOES

2 tablespoons CHOPPED, FRESH HERBS, E.G. THYME AND ROSEMARY

1 LEMON

Boil the rice with 200 ml water and 1/2 teaspoon salt.

Cut the cabbage leaves away from the stock. Parboil the leaves in boiling water for approx. 3 minutes. Take out and put in cold water.

Chop the shallots finely and mix with the mincemeat. Press in the garlic and crumble in the cheese. Work until smooth and season with salt and pepper.

Preheat the oven to 225 degrees. Portion the mincemeat on 12 leaves of savoy cabbage. Fold and roll. Grease an ovenproof dish and put in the stuffed cabbage leaves with the join downwards. Brush with the rest of the oil.

Pour the tomatoes and stock around the stuffed cabbage.

Wash and cut the potatoes in halves and add them to the dish. Sprinkle with herbs. Cook in the oven for approx. 35 minutes.

Cut the lemon into wedges and add these to the dish for the last 5 minutes.

On the day after the storm,
the air still carries the tang
of seaweed and salt.

lakes and seas

SALMON MARINATED IN LEMON THYME AND ELDERFLOWER

Marinating your own salmon to make gravlax is surprisingly easy. Besides, it is nice to be able to choose your own seasoning. This is a real early-summer salmon, with the taste of elderflower and herbs. Now, of course, elderflower cordial can be bought all the year round! Delicious with boiled new potatoes with a little cold-pressed rape-seed oil and the juice and gratings from a lemon.

6–8 HELPINGS

1 kg FILLETED SALMON WITH THE SKIN STILL ON

3 tablespoons SALT

1/2 tablespoon CRUSHED ROSÉ PEPPER

3 tablespoons LIQUID HONEY

4 tablespoons CONCENTRATED ELDERFLOWER CORDIAL

2 tablespoons FRESH LEMON THYME

Freeze the salmon for 1 day. Take out and thaw. Clean the salmon and remove any bones. Rub with salt and pepper. Pour the honey in coils and pour on the elderflower juice. Sprinkle with thyme.

It is practical to put the salmon in a big, thick plastic bag. Let the salmon lie cold for 3 days. Turn the bag occasionally.

Cut into thin slices.

BOILED PRAWNS

In the late summer and autumn wonderful prawns are caught off the west coast of Sweden. It is important to remember to boil the prawns correctly, so that they become tender and melt in the mouth. Prawns are delicious when eaten au naturel but also taste fabulous when cooked au gratin.

Wash the prawns in cold water. Bring water, beer, salt, sugar and dill to the boil.

Put in the prawns and let them boil 1–2 minutes.

Take out the prawns with a draining spoon.

Let the liquid and the prawns cool separately.

Put the prawns in the cold liquid and allow to soak for at least 4 hours.

2 kg PRAWNS

5 litres WATER

1 bottle (33 CL) DARK BEER

250 ml SALT

15 SUGAR CUBES

2 hg HEADS OF DILL

GRATINATED PRAWNS

Preheat the oven to 250 degrees. Chop the mushrooms and the onion finely.

Fry the mushrooms and onion in butter in a saucepan until the onion is transparent. Season with salt and pepper. Pour the fond, brandy and cream over and allow to reduce.

Grate the fresh bread and blend it into the mushroom mixture together with grated lemon peel and parsley.

Cut the prawns lengthwise and put them in an ovenproof dish with the cut side up.

Spoon the mushroom mixture over the prawns and top with the cheese.

Bake the prawns in the upper part of the oven for approx. 15 minutes, or until they turn golden. Serve with good bread and a salad.

SERVES 4 (AS A STARTER)

8 BOILED PRAWNS

200 g FRESH MUSHROOMS

1 SMALL ONION

2 tablespoons BUTTER

3 measuring spoons SALT

2 measuring spoons FRESHLY GROUND BLACK PEPPER

1 tablespoon LOBSTER FOND

2 tablespoons BRANDY

3 tablespoons CREAM

2 SLICES FRESH WHITE BREAD

1/2 teaspoon GRATED LEMON PEEL

50 ml CHOPPED FLAT-LEAF PARSLEY

100 ml GRATED MATURE CHEESE

SOTARE

Sotare is herring which is fried or grilled until it turns sooty. Delicious to eat newly barbecued at the seaside on a lovely summer's evening, with new potatoes and dill butter.

SERVES 4

16 HERRING

3 tablespoons RAPE-SEED OIL

3 teaspoons GOURMET SALT

Prepare a grill or use a large frying pan. Clean the fish but leave the backbones and the heads on.

Remove the scales by drawing a knife against them. Dry the fish and brush with oil and salt on both sides.

If you put the herring in a grill basket it makes them easier to handle.

Grill or fry them over high heat until they are completely sooty.

TURBOT WITH HORSERADISH

Turbot is a large flatfish which is wonderful to eat lightly boiled, together with fresh horseradish and melted butter. The tastiest accompaniment, of course, is newly boiled fresh potatoes. If it is not the season for turbot it can be replaced with, for example, cod back.

SERVES 4

600–800 g TURBOT, BONED WEIGHT

approx. 1 litre FISH STOCK

1 teaspoon SALT

100 g BUTTER

4–6 tablespoons FRESHLY GROUND HORSERADISH

200 g SUGAR PEAS

1.2 kg FRESH POTATOES

Boil up the fish stock and salt and add the fish. Take off the heat and allow to stand for 3–8 minutes, depending on how thick the fish is. The fish should be white inside when it is cooked. It is important not to boil for too long as this makes the fish dry.

Melt the butter by heating it and skim off the foam so that it is clear.

Serve with newly grated horseradish, boiled sugar peas and fresh potatoes.

SHRIMP SANDWICH

Shrimps suit most occasions. It is nicest to shell the shrimps yourself at the table and eat them with some really good bread and a tasty mix. In this way everyone can make their own open sandwich.

Butter the slices of bread. Clean the shrimps and put them on the bread.

Mix oil, salt, pepper and lemon in a small bowl. Fold in the dill.

Pour a coil of dill oil on each sandwich.

4 open sandwiches

3 tablespoons BUTTER

4 SLICES FARMHOUSE BREAD

6–8 hg FRESH SHRIMPS

100 ml RAPE-SEED OIL

1/2 teaspoon HERB SALT

2 measuring spoons LEMON PEPPER

1 tablespoon SQUEEZED LEMON + 1/2 TEASPOON GRATED LEMON PEEL

2 tablespoons CUT DILL

79

LOBSTER SALAD WITH ROOT VEGETABLES AND HORSERADISH AND CHANTERELLE CREAM

The tastiest way to eat newly boiled lobster is au naturel – and the same really applies to all fresh shellfish. But this delicious lobster salad with horse-radish and chanterelle cream is unforgettable too.

Take the meat out of the lobsters and cut it into pieces.

Melt the butter in a saucepan and put in the shredded vegetables to soften.

Put in the spinach, season and finally add lemon juice and grated lemon rind.

Chop the chanterelles finely and fry them in butter. Allow to cool.

Mix the chanterelles with crème fraîche and horseradish and season if necessary with salt and pepper.

Serve the meat from 1/2 lobster per person. Garnish with the mixture of spinach and root vegetables on the side and add a dollop of horse-radish and chanterelle cream.

SERVES 4

2 BOILED LOBSTERS

1 tablespoon BUTTER

2 tablespoons PEELED, SHREDDED CELERIAC

2 tablespoons PEELED, SHREDDED CARROT

2 tablespoons PEELED, SHREDDED SWEDE

20 FRESH SPINACH LEAVES

SALT AND PEPPER

2 tablespoons SQUEEZED LEMON + 1/2 TEASPOON GRATED LEMON RIND

HORSERADISH AND CHANTERELLE CREAM:

100 g FRESH CHANTERELLES

1 tablespoon BUTTER

100 ml CRÈME FRAÎCHE

2 tablespoons FINELY GRATED FRESH HORSERADISH

BOILED MUSSELS

On the west coast of Sweden fishermen catch mussels with their silvery shells and tasty contents. Mussels can be cooked in many ways, either boiled au naturel, baked au gratin or used in soups or stews.

1 kg

1 kg FRESH MUSSELS

1 ONION

1 GARLIC CLOVE (OPTIONAL)

1 tablespoon BUTTER

200 ml DRY WHITE WINE

200 ml WATER

1/2 teaspoon SALT

1/2 BUNCH FLAT-LEAF PARSLEY

Brush the mussel shells well and cut off the beards. Check that they are fresh by tapping the shell lightly. If the mussel closes then it is fresh.

Chop the onion and fry it in the butter in a sauté pan, with pressed garlic if desired, until transparent. Pour on wine and water, add salt and bring to the boil.

Put in the parsley.

Put in the mussels and boil covered for approx. 5 minutes, until all the mussels have opened. Throw away any mussels which have not opened.

Strain off the liquid and let the mussels cool, after which they can be taken out of their shells.

MUSSEL SOUP

Follow the recipe on the preceding spread, dilute with cream and added chopped parsley leaves.

If you want the soup a little thicker, stir in cornflour and bring to the boil.

SERVES 4

1 kg FRESH MUSSELS

1 ONION

1 GARLIC CLOVE (OPTIONAL)

1 tablespoon BUTTER

200 ml DRY WHITE WINE

200 ml WATER

1/2 teaspoon SALT

1/2 BUNCH FLAT-LEAF PARSLEY

100 ml CREAM

1–2 tablespoons CORNFLOUR

GRATINATED MUSSELS

Preheat the oven to 250 degrees.

Halve the boiled mussels and leave the mussel in one half.

Mix breadcrumbs, parsley, and the garlic, if desired, and spoon the mixture into the mussel shells. Drop a little oil on the mussels and top with the cheese.

Bake in an ovenproof dish for approx. 5 minutes in the upper part of the oven.

SERVES 4

1/2 BATCH OF BOILED MUSSELS (PAGE 46)

3 tablespoons BREADCRUMBS

3 tablespoons CHOPPED FLAT-LEAF PARSLEY

1 GARLIC CLOVE (OPTIONAL)

50 ml RAPE-SEED OIL

100 ml GRATED MATURE CHEESE

SHELLFISH SAUCE

In autumn the Swedish crabs are well-fed and tasty. The simplest way to enjoy them is with a classical mustard sauce and freshly baked blue cheese muffins.

Whisk the two kinds of mustard, the sugar, honey, vinegar and oil for the sauce in a small bowl. Finally, add the dill and let the sauce mature for a few hours before serving.

6 HELPINGS

2–3 tablespoons SWEET MUSTARD

1 teaspoon DIJON MUSTARD

2 tablespoons GRANULATED SUGAR

1 tablespoon HONEY

2 tablespoons WHITE WINE VINEGAR

100 ml RAPE-SEED OIL

3 tablespoons CHOPPED DILL

BLUE CHEESE MUFFINS

Preheat the oven to 225 degrees.

Melt the butter and let it cool slightly.

Mix the two kinds of flour, the salt and baking powder in a bowl.

Add egg, soured milk and crumbled blue cheese.

Pour the mixture over the dry ingredients and work up to a thick paste.

Spoon the paste into bun papers, filling them 2/3 full. Bake in the lower part of the oven for 15–20 minutes.

Serve as fresh as possible.

12 muffins

75 g BUTTER

200 ml GRAHAM FLOUR

400 ml FLOUR

1/2 teaspoon SALT

4 teaspoons BAKING POWDER

2 EGGS

200 ml SOURED MILK (FILMJÖLK)

100 g BLUE CHEESE

12 BUN PAPERS

Lie down on the jetty on an early summer's morning.
Lie still, perfectly still, with your ear against the warm plank.
Can you hear it? The lake is singing.

BOILED CRAYFISH

Even though crayfish are now sold all the year round, most Swedes probably still eat crayfish at least once in August every year. Few people have the privilege of enjoying fresh Swedish crayfish, but other kinds are available frozen to keep the tradition alive.

A tasty goat's cheese pie is a fine accompaniment.

1 kg

1 kg FRESH OR FROZEN CRAYFISH

2 1/2 litres COLD WATER

1 teaspoon GRANULATED SUGAR

50 ml SALT

1 ONION

5 HEADS OF DILL

If using live crayfish, make sure they are healthy by pulling out the tail, which should coil back if the shellfish is all right. If you have frozen crayfish, thaw them.

Boil water with sugar and salt in a large saucepan. Slice the onion and add it and the dill to the pan.

Put in the live crayfish and then boil for 10 minutes, or pour the hot liquid over the thawed crayfish.

Allow the crayfish to cool in the liquid in a cold place.

GOAT'S CHEESE PIE

APPROX. 6 SMALL PIES OR ONE BIG PIE

DOUGH:

125 g BUTTER

300 ml FLOUR

1 tablespoon COLD WATER

FILLING:

3 EGGS

100 ml CREAM

2 measuring spoons FRESHLY GROUND BLACK PEPPER

200 g GOAT'S CHEESE

1–2 tablespoons CHOPPED, FRESH ROSEMARY

2 tablespoons HONEY

Mix the butter and flour in a food processor with the chopping blade inserted, or by hand. Add the water and work quickly into a dough. Press out the dough in 6 individual pie dishes (or one large dish) and keep in a cool place for 30 minutes.

Preheat the oven to 225 degrees.

Indent the edge of the pie and prebake for 10 minutes in the middle of the oven.

Whisk the eggs and cream for the filling. Season with black pepper and crumble in the cheese.

Pour the filling into the pie shell and bake for approx. 20 minutes until the pie has "stopped".

Garnish with rosemary and pour coils of honey over it to serve.

WORMWOOD SCHNAPPS

On Saint Bartholomew's Day, 24 August, the fragrant, pale green wormwood should be harvested and then hung up to dry. The bitter schnapps will be excellent by next year's crayfish party.

1 litre ABSOLUT VODKA

2 tablespoons DRIED, STRIPPED WORMWOOD FLOWERS

Put the dried flowers in a small fireproof bowl. Pour on the wormwood flowers and 2 tablespoonfuls of vodka and burn with match. Pour on 50 ml spirits and allow to soak for a day. Strain off the flowers. Use then as a concentrate and dilute with spirits to the desired bitterness.

RASPBERRY MOUSSE

Since raspberries are ripe in the crayfish season, this dessert is particularly suitable after the crayfish.

SERVES 4

3 GELATINE SHEETS

200 g RASPBERRIES

3+3 tablespoons GRANULATED SUGAR

1 1/2 tablespoons WATER

2 EGGS

100 ml WHIPPED CREAM

Soak the gelatine sheets in cold water. Boil half of the raspberries together with 3 tablespoonfuls of sugar and water until they are slightly softened. Mash with a fork and leave to cool.

Whisk the eggs and the rest of the sugar until they are white and fluffy and fold into the crushed raspberries.

Bring the mixture to the boil over a low heat while stirring. Remove from the heat. Squeeze out the gelatine sheets and let them melt in the warm raspberry mixture. Leave to cool. Stir occasionally.

Whip the cream hard and fold it into the mousse.

Allow to stand cold for approx. 2 hours.

Spoon the mousse into attractive bowls and garnish with the rest of the raspberries.

MINCED PIKE BALLS

The pike is a fine freshwater fish which is unfortunately overshadowed by saltwater fish. These minced fish balls are easy to make and taste wonderful together with crayfish sauce, pressed potato and freshly boiled beans.

Mix the fish finely in a food processor with the chopping blade inserted. Fold in the cream carefully. Whisk the egg whites into a hard foam and fold them into the mixture. Season with salt and pepper. Put in a cool place for a while. Peel and boil the potatoes.

Melt the butter for the sauce in a pan, stir in the flour and the milk. Allow to boil together for 3–5 minutes, stirring frequently. Season with lobster fond, lemon and, if desired, with the water in which you have boiled crayfish. Finally, put in the crayfish and the spinach and let the sauce heat without boiling.

Shape the balls out of the minced fish and boil in lightly salted water for approx. 5 minutes. Press the potatoes and serve together with the sauce and the fish balls garnished with roe.

SERVES 4

400 g SKINNED AND BONED PIKE

300 ml CREAM

3 EGG WHITES

2 measuring spoons GROUND WHITE PEPPER

1/2 teaspoon SALT

approx. 12 FLOURY POTATOES

100 g WHITEFISH ROE

CRAYFISH SAUCE:

2 tablespoons BUTTER OR MARGARINE

3 tablespoons FLOUR

250 ml MILK

2 tablespoons LOBSTER FOND

1 tablespoon SQUEEZED LEMON

150 g PEELED CRAYFISH TAILS (MAY BE TINNED)

200 g FRESH SPINACH

SALMON CARPACCIO

Try my Swedish variant of the classical Italian carpaccio. This was originally made from fillet of veal but here I use salmon instead.

Since salmon carpaccio is easy to make in advance, it works well as a delicious starter. Freshly baked bread is a good accompaniment.

4–6 HELPINGS

500 g SKINNED AND BONED SALMON FILLET IN PIECES

1 teaspoon GOURMET SALT

1/2 teaspoon FRESHLY GROUND BLACK PEPPER

75 g MATURE CHEESE

100 ml SUNFLOWER SHOOTS

100 ml SUNFLOWER SEEDS

DRESSING:

2 tablespoons RASPBERRY VINEGAR

4 tablespoons RAPE-SEED OIL

2 tablespoons CHIVES

3 measuring spoons SALT

2 measuring spoons FRESHLY GROUND BLACK PEPPER

Put the salmon in the freezer for 2 days, so that any parasites in the raw fish disappear.

Let the salmon half-thaw in the refrigerator. It is then easiest to slice wafer-thin. Arrange nicely on a dish or plate.

Sprinkle with salt and pepper, cover with thin slices of cheese and top with sunflower shoots. Roast the sunflower seeds in a dry frying pan until they are slightly browned. Sprinkle over the salmon.

Whisk vinegar and oil for the dressing. Chop the chives and together with the spices for the dressing. Pour the dressing over the slices of salmon.

LIGHTLY SALTED COD WITH BEETROOT SAUCE, BLACK SALSIFY AND SUGAR PEAS

Lightly salting the cod makes its flesh firmer and whiter. Together with the beetroot sauce, the black salsify and the peas, the dish makes up a beautiful colour palette on the plate.

Rub the fish with salt and sugar and keep cold in a plastic bag for about 12 hours.

Preheat the oven to 200 degrees and put in the fish until the inner temperature is 55 degrees.

Peel and grate the beetroots and boil them until soft in approx. 200 ml lightly salted water. Pour off the water. Make into a smooth sauce in a mixer. Pour back into the saucepan and boil together with fond, vermouth and cream. Season with salt, sugar and white pepper.

Peel the black salsify, clean the leek and the sugar peas and cut them into smaller pieces. Boil the vegetables separately until they are only just soft. Pour off the water and turn them in a little butter in a saucepan.

Portion the dish to serve. Pour the sauce as a mirror on the plate, put the vegetables on top and finally the fish.

SERVES 4

600 g BONED COD BACK

1 1/2 tablespoons SALT

3/4 tablespoon GRANULATED SUGAR

3 FRESH BEETROOTS

1 teaspoon SALT

1 tablespoon CHICKEN FOND

1 tablespoon VERMOUTH (OPTIONAL)

50 ml COOKING CREAM

2 measuring spoons WHITE PEPPER

300 g BLACK SALSIFY

1/2 LEEK

200 g SUGAR PEAS

1 tablespoon BUTTER

in the garden

We spread a cloth in the shadow of the cherry tree.
All the rolls will soon be eaten but we stay there talking, almost whispering, as afternoon gives way to evening.

GRATED POTATO AND ARTICHOKE PANCAKES

Swedish rårakor are a tasty kind of pancakes usually made from grated potato, but they are in fact even more delicious with a little admixture of Jerusalem artichokes.

Here the potato pancakes are served with lovely whitefish roe to make a perfect starter or snack.

Peel the potatoes and artichokes and grate them on the coarse side of the grater.
Mix the potato and artichoke well and salt. Drop in a pan or griddle and fry them golden in butter. Arrange nicely on plates and add a dollop of crème fraîche and whitefish roe. Garnish with chives and serve at once.

SERVES 4

approx. 200 g (4–5) FLOURY POTATOES

approx. 200 g (6) JERUSALEM ARTICHOKES

1 teaspoon GOURMET SALT

3 tablespoons BUTTER

50 ml CRÈME FRAÎCHE

50 ml WHITEFISH ROE

CHIVE STALKS AS GARNISH

TOMATO CHUTNEY

Chutney goes well with various meat, poultry and fish dishes. Perhaps it is tastiest if the meat is grilled. Tomato chutney is also a fine accompaniment on a buffet or with cold cuts.

approx. 1 1/2 LITRES

16 RIPE TOMATOES

6 SHALLOTS

4 teaspoons CIDER VINEGAR

50 ml BROWN SUGAR

1/2 teaspoon GOURMET SALT

1/2 teaspoon YELLOW MUSTARD SEEDS

1–2 teaspoons FINELY CHOPPED CHILLI PEPPERS (N.B. THESE ARE HOT, SO USE CAREFULLY)

2 teaspoons FRESH GROUND GINGER

You can peel the tomatoes by dipping them in boiling water and then peeling them. I myself like the tough skin so I usually skip this. I also keep the cores.

Chop the tomatoes and the onion and mix with vinegar, brown sugar, salt, mustard seeds, chilli and ginger in a saucepan.

Allow to boil together while stirring for 10–15 minutes, or until the liquid has thickened. Place in bowls or jars. Chutney will keep in the refrigerator for several weeks.

MINT-MARINATED STRAWBERRIES WITH HONEY CREAM

The sweetness of strawberries and the freshness of mint make for an unbeatable combination. Here the marinated strawberries are accompanied by a honey cream as the perfect finishing touch.

SERVES 4

1 1/2 litre FRESH STRAWBERRIES

1/2 litre WATER

100 ml WHITE PORT

3 tablespoons WHITE SYRUP

approx. 20 LEAVES OF MINT

200 ml CRÈME FRAÎCHE

200 ml GOURMET QUARK

2 tablespoons HONEY, PREFERABLY LAVENDER HONEY

1 LIME

Clean the strawberries and divide them if they are big.

Bring the water, port and syrup to the boil. Chop 3/4 of the mint leaves and add to the pan.

Pour the warm liquid over the strawberries and leave to cool.

Mix crème fraîche, quark and honey. Grate the lime and mix in the rind and the juice.

Serve the strawberries cold with a dollop of honey cream. Garnish with mint.

ICED RHUBARB SOUP

For some reason I always think that rhubarb soup sounds so plain, although I know that is completely wrong. The soup is quite simply heavenly and refreshing after a filling meal.

Peel and cut the rhubarb into centimetre-long pieces, but save a length of about 10 cm for garnish.

Bring the water, wine and sugar to the boil and put in the centimetre-long pieces of rhubarb.

Bring to the boil again and the vanilla pod, divided lengthwise. Allow to boil for approx. 10 minutes. Shred the 10 cm piece of rhubarb and add to boil for the last 5 minutes.

Remove from the heat and allow to cool, first at room temperature and then in the refrigerator, preferably overnight.

Pour the quark in a bowl and crumble the meringues into it. Mix to a creamy consistency and put a dollop in each bowl of soup.

SERVES 4

300 g RHUBARB
500 ml WATER
200 ml DRY, WHITE WINE
150 ml SUGAR
1 VANILLA POD

CREAM:
250 g GOURMET QUARK
approx. 8 SMALL MERINGUES

HERRING CAKE

This cake with matjes herring is of course ideal for the Midsummer table but also as an appetizer or starter in many other situations. It is perfect for making in advance, particularly because it just gets tastier from maturing a day or two.

Cut the crust off the bread and chop it finely in a mixer with the chopping blade inserted. Cut the butter into cubes and add to the mixer. Mix until to a grainy consistency.

Press the mixture into a pie dish with a removable bottom, approx. 25 cm in diameter. Put in the refrigerator.

Soak the gelatine sheets in cold water. Chop the herring finely (save the liquid) and the red onion. Mix the herring and onion with quark and crème fraîche. Season with black pepper and the liquid from the herring. Squeeze the water out of the gelatine sheets and melt them over a low heat. Let the gelatine drip into the herring mixture and stir so that it does not get lumpy.

Spread the filling over the bread in the dish and leave in a cold place for at least 3 hours, preferably longer.

Garnish the cake with chives and radishes.

6–8 HELPINGS

BOTTOM:

200 g DARK RYE BREAD (KAVRING)

75 g BUTTER

FILLING:

4 GELATINE SHEETS

200 g MATJES HERRING

1 RED ONION

250 g GOURMET QUARK

200 ml CRÈME FRAÎCHE

1/2 teaspoon FRESHLY GROUND BLACK PEPPER

50 ml LIQUID FROM TINNED HERRING

GARNISH:

1 BUNCH CHIVES

1 BUNCH RADISHES

PICKLED HERRING

With its colourful accompaniments, pickled herring is a joy to behold and to taste.

200 ml DILUTED ACETIC ACID, 6%
150 ml GRANULATED SUGAR

1 TIN DRAINED HERRING FOR PICKLING
1 CARROT
1 RED ONION
1 SMALL LEEK
50 ml CHOPPED DILL
2 SMALL BAY LEAVES
5 CLOVES
1/2 tablespoon CRUSHED ALLSPICE CORNS
2 teaspoons YELLOW MUSTARD SEEDS

Mix the brine in a saucepan and bring to the boil while stirring so that the sugar dissolves. Leave to cool.

Rinse and clean the herring fillets and cut into nice pieces. Peel and clean the carrot, red onion and leek. Cut into pieces. Put all the ingredients in a jar and pour the brine over them.

Allow to stand cold for 2–3 days, preferably longer.

LEMON AND HORSE-RADISH MARINATED HERRING

This marinated herring is refreshing and tasty, a natural dish for the Midsummer table. Come to think of it, for Christmas and Easter as well...

400 g FILLETED HERRING

1 litre WATER

150 ml ACETIC ACID, 12%

3 1/2 tablespoons SALT

125 g FROMAGE FRAIS WITH HORSERADISH

100 ml CRÈME FRAÎCHE

1 LEMON

1/2 teaspoon SALT

2 measuring spoons FRESHLY GROUND BLACK PEPPER

1 tablespoon HONEY

1 tablespoon FRESH, GRATED HORSERADISH

Deep-freeze the fish for 1 day. Take out and thaw.

Mix water, acetic acid and 3 tablespoons salt to make the marinade. Put in the herrings and marinate for at least 8 hours, preferably longer.

Mix the fromage frais and crème fraîche in a bowl. Wash the lemon and grate the rind, and squeeze it. Mix with the sauce and season with salt, pepper, honey and horseradish.

Take out the herrings and pour off the liquid. Put them in the sauce and allow to mature, preferably overnight.

PANCAKES WITH BLACKBERRY

Thin, freshly made pancakes are a favourite dish among both children and adults. Pancakes are surely one of our national dishes in Sweden.

8–10 PANCAKES

150 ml FLOUR

300 ml MILK

200 ml WHIPPED CREAM

1/2 teaspoon SALT

1 teaspoon VANILLA SUGAR

4 EGGS

2 tablespoons BUTTER

FILLING:

150 ml WHIPPED CREAM

approx. 300 ml BLACKBERRIES

1 tablespoon ICING SUGAR

Whisk the flour and a little milk at a time so that the mixture does not get lumpy.

Add the cream, the salt, vanilla sugar and finally break in the eggs. Melt the butter and stir into the mixture or use it to grease the pan.

Bake the pancakes until they are golden on both sides.

Serve with whipped cream and fresh berries. Powder with icing sugar.

STEWED PLUMS WITH A DASH OF BRANDY

It's wonderful to have fruit trees in your own garden, but sometimes you don't know what to do with all the fruit. This compote is a highly appreciated and tasty reminder of the harvest, even when the late autumn damp sets in.

If you want to peel the plums first, dip them for a little while in boiling water. Pull off the peel. Halve the plums and remove the stones.

Boil up water, syrup, cinnamon stick and vanilla pod, cut lengthwise.

Put in the plums and lemon rind and bring to the boil but only just.

Remove from the heat and allow to cool slightly. Pour in brandy and put in a cold place until serving. To be served cold or lukewarm, ideally with a dab of ice cream.

SERVES 4

500 g PLUMS
200 ml WATER
200 ml WHITE SYRUP
1 CINNAMON STICK
1 VANILLA POD
GRATED RIND OF 1/2 LEMON
150 ml BRANDY
VANILLA ICE CREAM (optional)

If you listen carefully
you can hear the fruit fall.

SIMPLE APPLE CAKE

An apple cake should be easy to make, so that you can serve it often during the season. I grew up with unwhipped cream as an accompaniment to apple cake, but it is also good to serve whipped cream flavoured with Calvados, or – of course – vanilla custard or ice cream.

Preheat the oven to 150 degrees. Grease an ovenproof dish with a little of the butter. Peel, rinse and core the apples, and cut them in slices. Arrange the apples in an attractive pattern in the dish. Sprinkle with sugar, grated lemon rind and add some drops of Calvados if desired. Mix cinnamon, flour and breadcrumbs and spread the mixture in the dish. Slice the rest of the butter thinly and put on top, and scatter the almond flakes.

Bake in the middle of the oven 30–45 minutes, depending on how thick the layer of apples is. The apples should be soft when the cake is ready. Serve lukewarm.

SERVES 4

4–6 COOKING APPLES
50 g BUTTER
3 tablespoons RAW SUGAR
2 teaspoons GRATED LEMON RIND
1 tablespoon CALVADOS (OPTIONAL)
2 teaspoons GROUND CINNAMON
50 ml FLOUR
50 ml BREADCRUMBS
50 g ALMOND FLAKES

STRAWBERRY JAM WITH LEMON BALM

It's fun to make your own jam. What's more, the result is particularly enjoyable. A little jar of jam is also a nice present to bring along on a visit. Thanks to the jam sugar this strawberry jam is quick to make.

approx. 1 litre

700 ml FRESH STRAWBERRIES

1 PACKET JAM SUGAR

approx. 20 LEAVES OF FRESH LEMON BALM

Clean and rinse the strawberries well and select just really good berries. There is otherwise a risk that the jam will get mouldy quickly.

Bring the berries and jam sugar to the boil in a saucepan over a low heat. Allow to boil for approx. 5 minutes. Skim off.

Put in the lemon balm and then pour the jam into thoroughly cleaned jars. You can keep it in the refrigerator for a few weeks or freeze it in plastic containers.

CINNAMON BUNS

I don't think anyone can be too old to enjoy newly baked cinnamon buns along with a glass of cold milk. These buns are totally irresistible...

32 buns

50 g SWEET DOUGH YEAST
100 g BUTTER
400 ml MILK
100 ml WHITE SYRUP
2 measuring spoons SALT
approx. 1-1,2 litre FLOUR
FILLING:
8 tablespoons SOFTENED BUTTER
6 tablespoons GRANULATED SUGAR
4–6 teaspoons GROUND CINNAMON
TO BRUSH:
1 EGG
2 tablespoons CRUSHED LOAF SUGAR, CAN BE MULTICOLOURED
32 BUN PAPERS

Crumble the yeast in a bowl. Melt the butter in a saucepan, pour in the milk and heat until hot to the touch. Pour this mixture over the yeast and stir so that it is all properly dissolved. Add syrup, salt and flour, a little at a time, until the dough comes away from the edge of the bowl. Leave the dough to rise at room temperature away from draughts for 30 minutes.

Take out the dough and knead it until it is shiny and elastic. Divide the dough into two equal parts and roll them out into rectangles. Mix the filling and spread it on the rectangles.

Roll up each rectangle from the long side. Then cut each roll into 16 equal-sized pieces and place them in bun papers on two baking trays.

Allow to rise for a further 30 minutes. Preheat the oven to 250 degrees.

Brush the buns with whisked egg and sprinkle with crushed loaf sugar. Bake each tray in the middle of the oven for approx. 6–8 minutes. The buns are ready when they are coloured even on the bottom.

CURD CAKE WITH CURRANTS

Curd cake is an old-fashioned dessert which used to be made from cheese rennet. This variant is instead made with cottage cheese, which makes it both tasty and slightly less fatty. When served with fresh currants in large quantities the sweet and the sour are a perfect match.

Preheat the oven to 175 degrees. Grease a wide ovenproof dish of approx. 2 l, or 4 individual dishes.

Blanch, peel and chop the almonds coarsely.

Whisk the eggs and sugar until they are white and fluffy. Fold in flour, milk, cottage cheese and almonds. Pour into the dish and bake in the middle of the oven for approx. 40 minutes, depending on how wide the dish is. The cake should have stagnated when it is ready.

Allow to cool slightly and decorate with the berries. Serve crème fraîche mixed with quark and vanilla sugar in a bowl alongside.

SERVES 4

1 tablespoon BUTTER OR MARGARINE

100 ml SWEET ALMONDS

3 EGGS

75 ml GRANULATED SUGAR

50 ml FLOUR

300 ml MILK

500 g NATURAL COTTAGE CHEESE

300 g REDCURRANTS

200 ml LIGHT CRÈME FRAÎCHE

150 ml GOURMET QUARK

1/2 teaspoon REAL VANILLA SUGAR

WILD STRAWBERRY PASTRIES

The very first wild strawberries, together with home-made vanilla cream and a fluffy sponge base ... A separate pastry for each guest feels extra festive.

4 buns

BOTTOM:

3 EGGS

150 ml SUGAR

200 ml FLOUR

1 teaspoon BAKING POWDER

25 g ALMOND FLAKES

FILLING:

300 ml CREAM

2 EGGYOLKS

1 tablespoon GRANULATED SUGAR

1 tablespoon POTATO FLOUR

2 teaspoons VANILLA SUGAR

300 ml FRESH WILD STRAWBERRIES AS GARNISH

OVEN PAPER

Preheat the oven to 250 degrees. Fold oven paper to line a baking tray.

Whisk the eggs and sugar until fluffy and then fold in flour and baking powder. Spread on the oven paper and scatter with the almonds.

Bake in the centre of the oven for approx. 5 minutes. Remove from the oven and turn the cake out on to oven paper. Brush the paper with a little cold water if the cake does not come loose. Cut out 8 circles using a glass.

Mix all the ingredients for the filling in a stainless steel saucepan, apart from the vanilla sugar and berries. Simmer the cream over a low heat, stirring all the time so that it does not curdle. Allow to cool. Stir occasionally. Put the bottoms together two by two with cream and wild strawberries between, and garnish with wild strawberries.

LINGONBERRY PEAR

Pears boiled in lingonberries (cowberries) are extremely decorative on a dessert plate because of their bold red colour.

They are also very tasty.

SERVES 4

4 RIPE PEARS

500 g LINGONBERRY COMPOTE

150 ml WATER

200 ml WHIPPED CREAM

1 tablespoon ARRACK PUNCH

Peel the pears and core them with an apple corer, from the bottom so that they look intact with the stalk still on them.

Boil the lingonberries with the water and add the pears. Cover and boil until soft, approx. 20 minutes.

Keep in a cool place until the following day.

Whip the cream and add some arrack punch. Put a pear on each plate and add a dollop of cream beside it.

in the forest

The tops of the spruce trees whisper and sough, but far beneath the tussocks lie still.

The forest is an enchanted world, at once secretive and smiling.

We tread carefully over the moss and fill our baskets with the gifts of the ground.

ELDERFLOWER CORDIAL

The creamy coloured flowers of the elder blossom in June–July and they are easy to pick. Elderflower cordial can be made quickly and is also tasty to mix with cold white wine or perhaps even a little vodka, to give a stronger drink.

Rinse the flowers. Bring the water, sugar, sliced lemon and citric acid to the boil. Pour this over the elderflowers and allow to stand for 5 days. Strain through a cloth and pour into thoroughly cleaned bottles. Freeze in plastic containers for longer storage.

APPROX. 4 LITRES

60 CLUSTERS OF ELDERFLOWER
3 litres WATER
3 litres GRANULATED SUGAR
3 LEMONS
100 g CITRIC ACID

LINGONBERRY JAM

In the early autumn the dark red, slightly bitter lingonberries (cowberries) ripen in our Swedish forests. The berries are excellent for making jam, and since the jam keeps very well, it suits many different uses during the year. Perhaps the best-known combination is lingonberries and meatballs.

Clean the berries well so that they are free of stalks and leaves. Rinse them.

Put the berries, water and sugar in a saucepan and boil while stirring for approx. 20 minutes. The berries should become slightly mushy.

Pour into thoroughly cleaned jars and the jam will keep in the refrigerator until the next autumn.

APPROX. 1 LITRE JAM

1 kg FRESH LINGONBERRIES

200 ml WATER

600 ml SUGAR

ELK STEW WITH ROOT VEGETABLE COMPOTE

In autumn the hunting season for elk or moose starts in much of Sweden. This means that fresh elk meat is now available in many shops, just as there can be funnel chanterelles at the vegetable counter. I am fortunate enough to be able to go to Småland every autumn and pick the mushrooms myself. Funnel chanterelles are good for drying, so that you can enjoy them the whole year round.

Cut away any membranes and clean the meat. Brown the meat in the butter in a pot, preferably of cast iron.

Peel the onions, add them to the pot and brown them slightly. Pour on the water and allow to boil under cover for approx. 20 minutes.

Put in the chanterelles. Season with gin, fond, lingonberries and salt and pepper. Peel and slice the carrots and cook them until soft in the stew. If you want a thicker sauce, add a little potato flour stirred in cold water.

Peel the potatoes and parsnips and cut them into pieces.

Boil in lightly salted water until soft, approx. 20 minutes. Add butter and cream and mash them. The mash should still be a bit chewy, not too fine. Season.

Chop the parsley and add it last to the mash.

Serve the stew with the root vegetable compote and lingonberry jam.

SERVES 4

600 g STEWING STEAK OF ELK

2 tablespoons BUTTER OR MARGARINE

10 SMALL ONIONS

200 ml WATER

200 ml FRESH FUNNEL CHANTERELLES OR EQUIVALENT, DRIED

2 tablespoons GIN

1 tablespoon GAME FOND

2 tablespoons LINGONBERRY JAM + A LITTLE TO GARNISH

SALT AND PEPPER

3 CARROTS

1–2 tablespoons POTATO FLOUR (OPTIONAL)

ROOT VEGETABLE COMPOTE:

6 POTATOES

1–2 PARSNIPS

1 tablespoon BUTTER

100 ml COOKING CREAM

SALT AND PEPPER

2 tablespoons FLAT-LEAF PARSLEY

We have almost given up hope when the glade opens in front of us.
We cautiously crouch down and shove the leaves away.
And here, in the shelter of the thick mossy carpet,
marches the forest's own little army of pale yellow hats.

MARINATED CHANTERELLES

Either you have no chanterelles at all, or else you have too many at once! Anyway, this is a really good way to enjoy the delicious pale yellow mushrooms.

Marinated chanterelles are a delicacy for the buffet or as an accompaniment to meat and poultry dishes.

3 SHALLOTS

2 tablespoons RAPE-SEED OIL

1 CLOVE OF GARLIC

300 g CHANTERELLES

1 measuring spoon FRESH THYME

2 measuring spoons FRESH TARRAGON

100 ml CIDER VINEGAR

50 ml WATER

1 teaspoon SUGAR

Peel and chop the onion. Fry until transparent in oil in a saucepan.

Press in the garlic. Clean the mushrooms and cut them if they are big. Add them to the pan and let them fry a short while. Season with thyme and tarragon. Pour in vinegar and water and raw sugar and allow to boil together for a few minutes.

Allow to cool and then keep in jars in a cold place.

BLUEBERRY MUFFINS

These muffins are easy to make, which is good luck because they are so tasty that they tend to disappear quickly. Go out and pick fresh blueberries in the forest's own pantry, or use other berries depending on the season.

APPROX. 12 MUFFINS

950 ml FLOUR

250 g BLUEBERRIES

2 EGGS

250 ml MILK

250 ml SOURED MILK (FILMJÖLK)

200 g SOFTENED BUTTER

250 ml GRANULATED SUGAR

1/2 teaspoon SALT

1/2 tablespoon BAKING POWDER

12 LARGE MUFFIN PAPERS

Preheat the oven to 175 degrees.

Mix 50 ml of the flour with the berries so that they will not sink so easily to the bottom of the muffins.

Whisk the eggs, milk, soured milk and softened butter together.

Mix flour, sugar, salt and baking powder in a bowl. Pour in the egg mixture and the berries and stir carefully.

Spoon the mixture into the bun papers so that they are almost full. Bake in the bottom half of the oven for approx. 25 minutes. Feel with a needle – if it is dry the muffins are ready.

ROAST VENISON WITH GRATINATED ROOT VEGETABLES

In the autumn and winter months well-stocked shops offer different kinds of game. The exact range varies depending on which part of Sweden you are in. Here I have a recipe for roast elk but you can substitute roe deer or red deer. If it is difficult to obtain venison, beef will also do.

Preheat the oven to 175 degrees.

Cut away any membranes on the meat and rub it with salt, pepper and crushed juniper berries.

Put in an ovenproof dish and cut pieces of onion and carrot to arrange around it. Stick in a meat thermometer at the thickest part of the roast.

Peel and cut all the vegetables into thin slices. This is easiest in a food processor with the slicing disc inserted.

Peel and chop the onion. Grease an ovenproof dish.

Alternate the different root vegetables and onion in the dish. Salt and pepper between the layers.

Pour over the cream and place in the oven, 40–60 minutes. The time depends on how thick the layers are. Test with a needle to feel whether the vegetables are soft.

When approx. 10 minutes is left, strew the thyme leaves and the cheese on the top.

Read the thermometer in the roast, which should show approx. 62 degrees when it is ready. If you want it well done let it stand a little longer.

Let the roast rest under foil for a while and then carve it in fine slices and serve along with the gratinated vegetables.

SERVES 6–8

approx. 1.2 kg ELK ROAST
1 teaspoon SALT
4 measuring spoons FRESHLY GROUND BLACK PEPPER
5 CRUSHED JUNIPER BERRIES
1 ONION
1 CARROT

GRATINATED ROOT VEGETABLES:
6 POTATOES
1 SMALL SWEDE, approx. 200 g
1 BIT PARSNIP, approx. 150 g
2 CARROTS
1 BIT CELERIAC, approx. 75 g
1 ONION
2 tablespoons BUTTER
2 teaspoons HERB SALT
3 measuring spoons FRESHLY GROUND BLACK PEPPER
100-200 ml COOKING CREAM
1 tablespoon CHOPPED, FRESH THYME LEAVES
200 ml GRATED MATURE CHEESE

When the chill begins to bite through wool, its time to go indoors.

The soup on the stove, the mittens in a neat pile on the radiator.

indoors

MEATBALLS

Meatballs are probably one of the most Swedish of dishes. They are just as suitable on the buffet as sliced on a piece of bread – and as a main course, with all the classic accompaniments: sauce, potatoes and lingonberry jam. Best washed down with a big glass of cold milk!

SERVES 4

400 g MINCEMEAT, MIXED PORK AND BEEF

2 MEDIUM-SIZED BOILED POTATOES

50 ml MILK

1 tablespoon FINELY GRATED ONION

1 teaspoon SALT

2 measuring spoons FRESHLY GROUND WHITE PEPPER

1 EGG

2 tablespoons BUTTER

SAUCE:

2 tablespoons FLOUR

400 ml WATER

1 tablespoon MEAT FOND

100 ml COOKING CREAM

1/2 teaspoon SOY SAUCE

SALT AND PEPPER

Put the mincemeat in a bowl. Grate or mash the potatoes and mix in together with the milk, onion and spices. Finally, add the egg.

Work the mixture until smooth and then shape the balls to the desired size.

Fry the meatballs in butter in a frying pan until they are golden. Sprinkle the flour in the pan in the remaining fat. Pour in the water, a little at a time, while stirring. Bring to the boil and stir occasionally so that the sauce does not get lumpy. Flavour with fond and cream. Add the soy sauce for colour. Allow to boil for 3–5 minutes and season at the end with salt and pepper, if necessary.

Serve with boiled potatoes, boiled carrots and lingonberry jam.

BOKEN OM PIPPI

GINGER SNAPS

Ginger snaps are part of Christmas in Sweden, and of course it is extra nice to enjoy them if they are baked with your own dough.
The traditional shapes of ginger snaps – the heart, the star, the goat – are varied here with Astrid Lindgren's now internationally known story figures.

Melt butter, sugar and light syrup in a saucepan.

Pour into a bowl or a large food processor and add all the spices, the bicarbonate and the egg.

Work in the flour until you have a sticky dough and leave to stand cold overnight.

Preheat the oven to 200 degrees. Roll out the dough on a floured board and cut out figures.

Place them on the baking tray with slight spaces between them and bake for approx. 5–7 minutes, depending on the thickness. Keep an eye on them as they burn easily.

Allow to cool on a rack. Store in an airtight container.

approx. 200 ginger snaps

150 g BUTTER
200 ml GRANULATED SUGAR
150 g LIGHT SYRUP
1 1/2 teaspoons GROUND GINGER
1 1/2 teaspoons GROUND CLOVES
1 teaspoon GROUND CINNAMON
1 teaspoon BICARBONATE
1 EGG
800 ml FLOUR

KALE SOUP

The kale should preferably be frostbitten to be really tasty. Chances of frost are good, as kale grows on the bare fields just before Christmas.

SERVES 4

1 ONION

1 1/2 tablespoons BUTTER

300 g STRIPPED, FRESH KALE

600 ml CHICKEN OR VEGETABLE STOCK

SALT AND PEPPER

100 g SMOKED HAM OR CHRISTMAS HAM

100 ml CRÈME FRAÎCHE

1 tablespoon BRANDY

Peel and chop the onion. Brown slightly in the butter in a saucepan.

Strip the kale leaves and rinse well.

Put the kale in the pan, pour on the stock and let it all boil for approx. 20 minutes.

Pour the soup into a large food processor with the chopping blade inserted and mix it, or use a blender.

Adjust the seasoning with salt and pepper.

Chop the ham finely and mix with crème fraîche. Salt and pepper and flavour with brandy.

Serve the soup piping hot with a dab of ham mousse in it.

After midnight the embers in the fire start to fade.

But the stars have better patience.

They stay together with the moon to meet the dawn.

LUCIA BUNS

Sneaking footsteps, whispering voices ... On the midwinter morning of the thirteenth of December we get up early to hail Lucia, the queen of light, with newly baked Lucia buns.

Soak the raisins in the mulled wine so that they will not burn so easily in the baking.

Crumble the yeast in a bowl. Melt the butter and pour in the milk. Let it get warm to the touch. Pour the liquid ingredients over the yeast and stir so that it is properly dissolved.

Add the quark, saffron, sugar, baking powder and work in a little of the flour at a time until the dough cleans the bowl. Leave to rise at room temperature away from draughts for approx. 45 minutes. Take out and knead the dough until it is shiny and without cracks.

Divide the dough into two equal-sized pieces and roll each piece into a thick oblong roll. Cut each roll into 8 equal-sized pieces.

Knead each bun until it is smooth and roll out to a narrow string. Then twist one end in a tail anticlockwise and one clockwise so that the coils meet in the middle.

Put on oven paper on a baking tray and press a raisin into the centre of each coil. Allow to rise for a further 30 minutes.

Preheat the oven to 225 degrees.

Whisk an egg and brush the buns carefully. Bake in the middle of the oven for approx. 8–10 minutes, until they are golden and feel hollow when you tap them on the bottom. Allow to cool on a rack under a cloth.

16 BUNS

50 ml RAISINS

3 tablespoons MULLED WINE

25 g FRESH SWEET DOUGH YEAST

75 g BUTTER

250 ml MILK

4 tablespoons GOURMET QUARK

1/2–1 g SAFFRON

100 ml GRANULATED SUGAR

1 teaspoon BAKING POWDER

700–800 ml FLOUR

1 EGG TO BRUSH WITH

SPRAT ROLL

The combination of Swedish-style anchovies, which are really spiced tinned sprat fillets, with onion and egg feels archetypically Swedish. In this new interpretation it is a suitable snack or starter, ideally accompanied by a fresh potato salad.

4–6 HELPINGS

OMELETTE:

50 g BUTTER

100 ml FLOUR

150 ml WHIPPED CREAM

300 ml MILK

3 EGGS

1/2 teaspoon BAKING POWDER

2 tablespoons JUICE FROM TINNED SPRATS

FILLING:

100 g ANCHOVY-STYLE SPRAT FILLETS

2 RED ONIONS

1 tablespoon BUTTER

100 ml CHOPPED PARSLEY

50 g GRATED MATURE CHEESE

POTATO SALAD:

5 ALMOND POTATOES

50 ml RAPE-SEED OIL

1 tablespoon CIDER VINEGAR

2 tablespoons LEMON JUICE + RIND OF ONE LEMON

3 tablespoons CHOPPED CHIVES

SALT AND PEPPER

OVEN PAPER

Preheat the oven to 250 degrees. First make the omelette.

Melt the butter in a saucepan and stir in the flour. Add the cream and milk gradually and allow to boil while stirring for approx. 3 minutes.

Crack the eggs and fold the yolks into the mixture. Keep the whites.

Stir in the baking powder and the juice from the tinned sprats and stir until smooth.

Whisk the egg whites into a hard foam and fold gently into the mixture.

Fold oven paper into a tray and grease it. Spread the mixture and bake in the middle of the oven for approx. 20 minutes. Turn out on oven paper and leave to cool.

In the meantime chop the sprats and the onion. Fry the onion in butter. Mix sprats and onion with parsley and cheese.

Spread the filling on the cooled omelette and roll up like a Swiss roll.

Scrub the potatoes and boil until they are only just soft. Slice them and put them in a bowl. Mix oil, vinegar, lemon juice and lemon rind and chives and pour over the potatoes. Season with salt and pepper.

LENTEN BUNS

Shrove Tuesday comes in February, when it is customary to eat cream buns in Sweden. In some parts of Sweden there is a tradition of eating "hot wedge", that is, cream buns served in bowls with warm milk.

Melt the butter in a saucepan, add the milk and heat until it is warm to the touch.

Crumble the yeast in a bowl. Add the liquid ingredients and stir so that the yeast is dissolved. Mix in the quark, sugar and salt.

Mix baking powder and flour. Add the flour mixture a little at a time until the dough cleans the bowl. Be careful not to use too much flour or the buns will be compact and dry.

Leave the dough to rise in the bowl at room temperature away from draughts for approx. 30 minutes.

Take out the dough and knead it until shiny and elastic. Cut in two parts and shape each piece into a roll. Cut 10 equal-sized buns from each roll and shape into round buns.

Put on a baking tray lined with oven paper and allow to rise for a further 30 minutes.

Preheat the oven to 225 degrees.

Brush the buns with whisked egg and bake in the middle of the oven for approx. 8–10 minutes. The buns should have turned a golden colour and should sound hollow when tapped on the bottom. Allow to cool for a while on a rack under a cloth.

Cut off a lid on each bun. Put a slice of almond paste in between and top with whipped cream.

Put on the lid and powder with icing sugar.

20 buns

100 g BUTTER

400 ml MILK

50 g FRESH SWEET DOUGH YEAST

100 ml QUARK

100 ml GRANULATED SUGAR

2 measuring spoons SALT

1 teaspoon BAKING POWDER

1-1,2 litre FLOUR

1 EGG

approx. 200 g ALMOND PASTE

200–300 ml WHIPPED CREAM

3 tablespoons ICING SUGAR

PEA SOUP

A bowl of steaming pea soup on a chilly winter's day is something most people appreciate. The soup is easy to make, just as long as you plan in advance and can stay at home while the soup is boiling.

A mug of warm arrack punch is a good accompaniment.

SERVES 4

TO SOAK:

500 ml DRIED YELLOW PEAS

2 litres WATER

2 tablespoons SALT

TO BOIL:

1 1/2 litre WATER

1/2 teaspoon SALT

1 ONION

2 teaspoons FRESH THYME + FOR DECORATION

300 g SMOKE-CURED LOIN OF PORK (KASSLER)

Rinse the peas in cold water and then put them in 2 l water, mixed with 2 tablespoons of salt. Allow to stand and soak overnight. Pour off the water.

Boil the soaked peas in lightly salted water with 1 peeled onion. Add fresh thyme and boil together with the whole piece of pork for approx. 1 1/2 hours.

Take out the pork and cut in strips.

Season with more salt if needed and dilute with water if the soup has thickened.

Serve with pork strips and fresh thyme.

INDEX OF RECIPES

measuring spoon = 1 ml
teaspoon = 5 ml
tablespoon = 15 ml

Margareta Schildt-Landgren is perhaps best known for her articles on food in the magazine Femina, to which she has been contributing for eleven years. She also writes in several other food magazines and monthlies.
Margareta has a background as a home economics teacher and has also been in charge of the experimental kitchen at the sugar company Sockerbolaget.
This is Margareta's third cookbook published by Kakao Förlag.
Margareta's book on accompaniments, Tillbehörsboken, won first prize in the category "Best Swedish Recipe" in the International Cookbook Awards, 2000.

Tine Guth-Linse has worked above all with features on interior decoration and food. She takes photographs for ICA Förlaget and magazines including Femina, Elle and Lantliv. Tine has worked at the International Center of Photography in New York and has studied photography and art history at Lund University.